COLUMBIA COLLEGE CHICAGO

3 2711 00160 9464

W9-CLN-921

DATE DUE

WITHDRAWN

Demco, Inc. 38-293

JUN 2 3 2009

Photographing Eden

COLUMBIA COLLEGE LIBRARY
600 S. MICHIGAN AVENUE
CHICAGO, IL 60605

Photographing Eden

poems

Jason Gray

OHIO UNIVERSITY PRESS

ATHENS

Ohio University Press, Athens, Ohio 45701
www.ohio.edu/oupress
www.ohioswallow.com
© 2008 by Ohio University Press
All rights reserved

To obtain permission to quote, reprint, or otherwise reproduce or distribute material
from Ohio University Press publications, please contact our rights and permissions
department at (740) 593-1154 or (740) 593-4536 (fax).

Printed in the United States of America
Ohio University Press books are printed on acid-free paper ♾ ™

16 15 14 13 12 11 10 09 08   5 4 3 2 1

Library of Congress Cataloging-in-Publication Data
Gray, Jason, 1976–
  Photographing Eden : poems / Jason Gray.
      p. cm.
  ISBN 978-0-8214-1835-2 (hc : alk. paper) — ISBN 978-0-8214-1836-9 (pbk. : alk.
paper)
  I. Title.
  PS3607.R3947P56 2008
  811'.6—dc22

                              2008044047

Acknowledgments

Grateful thanks to the editors of the following journals for their attention to my work:

The American Poetry Review: "Atlantis" and "Crossing the Border"

Barrow Street: "Memento Amori" and "Stone Goddess"

Image: "My Daughter as the Angel Gabriel in the Tableau Vivant of Van Grap's *Annunciation*"

Iron Horse Literary Review: "The Little Sphinx"

The Kenyon Review: "Letter to the Unconverted"

Literary Imagination: "Adam's Tongue"

The National Poetry Review: "Sciomancy"

Poetry: "The Snow Leopard"

Poetry Ireland Review: "Bear"

The Prague Revue: "The Snow Globe of Drowning Bears"

River Styx: "Circus Circus"

The Sewanee Theological Review: "The Nature Trail"

Smartish Pace: "A Generic Pietà," "The Old Balladeer Retires...," and "You Put Your Right Hand In, You Take Your Left Hand Out"

32 Poems: "Chagall in Heaven"

The Threepenny Review: "Adam & Eve Go to the Zoo"

"Adam & Eve Go to the Zoo" and "The Snow Leopard" were reprinted in the anthology *And We the Creatures* (Dream Horse Press, 2003). "Tower of Babel" was reprinted in *FlatCity* (FlatCity Press, 2005). "Adam & Eve Go to the Zoo" and "Tower of Babel" were reprinted on *Verse Daily.*

"A Field Guide to the Dark," "Photographing Eden," "Polar Bear at the Edge of a Hole in the Ice," and "Tower of Babel" first appeared in the chapbook *Adam & Eve Go to the Zoo* (Dream Horse Press, 2003).

"Adam Gifts Eve with a Session of Boudoir Photography," "Chiaroscuro," "Hey, You've Got to Hide Your Love Away," and "Meditations of the Tomb Painters" first appeared in the chapbook *How to Paint the Savior Dead* (Kent State University Press, 2007).

Thank you—

Kathy Fagan, Ben Howard, Andrew Hudgins, John Irwin, Mark Jarman, Lee Martin, Erin McGraw, Susan Morehouse, Eric Pankey, Paul Strong, Ellen Bryant Voigt, and Greg Williamson. Beth Bachmann, Michelle Burke, Dan Groves, Cynthia Hoffman, Hailey Leithauser, Alexander Long, Heather Price, Natalie Shapero, Ida Stewart, and Jen Town.

The Ohio State University Creative Writing Program, the Writing Seminars of Johns Hopkins University, and the English department of Alfred University. The Sewanee Writers' Conference and the Maryland State Council of the Arts.

Andrew and Erin, again thanks.

David Sanders and the staff of Ohio University Press. And Heather McHugh, who will have my lifelong gratitude.

—God bless.

http://jason-gray.net

To my nephew Oliver and the whole family

Contents

/

Yet one looks out
in an early morning hour such as this one,
watching a sparkling grackle land
upon a roof, and one imagines noon,
when every object clarifies itself
in sunlight, void of mind and shadow,
and is itself alone, a thick
beak, or iridescent wing.

—Ben Howard

A *Field Guide to the Dark*

Splice together both ends of the same wire.
You've tied off an empty circle,
A collar for Argos, and his leash will be
Strands of black hair knotted at your wrist.

He's as old as you feel, so let him guide you
Through field and forest, shadows gray, black,
And the dark's own phosphorescence,
The excited glow slowly fading out,

But not until you've followed it inward,
To a depression, dry as a sea-less bed,
The place familiar, but vantaged from
A distance before, as if a painting.

The wind is exhausted and collapses,
And you'd hope for stars, but not here,
The kingdom of the static, on the stoop
Of a white house gone blue in the dark.

Come in to the house where anger
Rests like a dinner plate on the edge
Of a table, and melancholy is the glass
Doorknob in and out of every room.

Sit down, sit down at the table with its
Pale yellow cloth (are those tiny flowers?)
And let your eyes adjust, for now that you've sat,
You'll be sitting here for a very long time.

The First Mermaid

Durham Castle

Her dress, full net of catch, curves to her right,
And her hair is a brimming bucket tipped aside.
No flippers here on this first mermaid carving,
Atop a column inside a disused chapel,
Covered by coal, then mocked by bicycles.
Forgotten, no longer even legend, she is
A Saxon joke inside a Norman church,
The hybrid dream of a lonely fisherman
Appropriated for a work that he
Was never destined for. He idles back
To his old boat, tricks the sea god used to play
Across the hours of empty line in water.
Little inventions, as he thinks of fish
And of his wife, and lets them drift together.
A Galatea or an Arethusa,
She is what he no longer has to see,
Chipping away at stone to make the church.
One day she must have set her mind to try on
This skirt of sea, and through it pushed her legs,
And when she caught it at her hips, no legs
Appeared again. A Venus in reverse,
She dove into the foam, troubling first
The surface, and then the sea closed in around her.
All this, the fisherman thought up
In the dark hall converting stone to art,
And that she didn't drown, but waved her tail—
Her new form freeing but already starting
To freeze into an icon—and splashed the water,
Making ripples which somewhere else are waves.

Running with My Father

Gone fat from grief, I took my heavy jar
And followed him in the high summer heat
For weeks to pare away the weight of loss
That hung around me like a planet's rings.
I had to lose my gravity. We ran
Our course until I easily outpaced him,
Searching for shade in the temporary leaves.

Up the hill now, a butterfly of sweat
On both our chests. What if his muscles give
Out in the days ahead? One loss recedes
Into another in the arc of sun.
My shadow falls behind. With invisible thread
I'm pulling him to the finish where ticker tape
Flies through the air as if it had no end.

Circus Circus

This is the trapeze a dream might make —
Precarious height from which you swing to safety
Or fall into your life, the swollen sea
Of calliope music where no drift net lies.
Blessed to land on solid ground for once
Instead of sinking deeper into the whirlpool
Where you are phase-shifted to some Middle Europe
With its klaxon angels that scream at you to wake.
Their dissonance overwhelms, like slides
Of all your human failures stacked together.
Try forgetting, and life will send its lions
To ravage the hole you make — so wide,
It is a flaming hoop. See how they leap
Through to the past, that sewer that does not drain?
Photograph what you see to freeze the moments
And watch the way the light betrays
Its very gift by fading. Even the light can't bear
The repeating, a scratch against the silence, the record
Never getting to where you want it to go,
But always in motion. The Big Top's shadow stretches
Across the grass and changes every second,
Like a sundial, but you refuse to see it,
Hiding beneath your never-unmade bed.

The Snow Leopard

In the Metro Toronto Zoo

For Paul Strong

He pads on grassy banks behind a fence,
with measured paces slow and tense.

Beyond his cage his thoughts are sharp and white;
he lives a compelled anchorite.

A solid ghost gone blind with all the green,
he waits and waits to be unseen.

Chiaroscuro

It's imperceptible, the line where light
Transforms to dark, or where awake becomes
Asleep, alone in the bed with dawn around
The bend of Christ's head in Caravaggio's
The Taking of Christ, hung up as a copy
Until the grime and age were cleaned away.
He's the master of *chiaroscuro,*
The slide from dark to light—this criminal,
On the run for most of his career from one
Rage or another, named in honor of
The angel Michael, brandishing a brush.
All crimes are done in dark, all crimes will meet
The light, says Christ, who suffered too at night—
The scent of anemone sent up with prayer,
The incensed guards approach in twos and then
Engulf him. The troubled sleepers raise their swords,
But in the end, who will sleep well this night?
Perhaps it's a gift for you, the long nights where
You know nothing but imponderable ache:
To be given dark, to face it when it fills
The bed, because so much will be withdrawn
From life, so much and not enough. And Christ,
Who knows the night's for kissing, pities you,
And knows the gradient you live upon.
To be given dark, the shadows on the wall
Like iron grillwork of a stair you can't
Decide to take or not, but then it's only
Gray and seamless wall. All our crimes are done
And there's the mundane miracle of the sun.

Adam & Eve Go to the Zoo

It is Adam who stops at the front gate
Even though it's open and held back.
He quivers as if he's thought of a splinter.
Eve is already looking past the iron gates
Into the plotted wilderness that aches
Inside of her like a vague déjà vu.

There is the walrus, there is the fox,
There is the panda and his hiding box.

Adam is drawn to bears: the bloated mass
Of brown fur, heavy-pawed. He feels this way:
Without dexterity. Yet Adam is
In awe of the secret nimbleness their fingers
And his contain. He wonders if someone, maybe
Even Eve, will ask to see how they work.

Eve finds herself pressed against the glass
Of the gorilla, bigger than she,
Whom she imagines she could fit inside,
The swell of child, or the ultraviolet
Blossom of soul. She hopes that maybe the bee
Will see what is beyond her vision now.

Here is the goat, here is the lamb,
Here is the camel with his head in the sand.

Here is Adam in the butterfly
Enclosure, disappointed by the silence.
Eve comes upon him here, and the monarchs come
And nest in her hair. She feels as if the wind
Has visited her; and Adam takes one on
His finger and lets Eve give it lift with breath.

The nursery, at last: egg-white and full
Of murmur; the cub is suckling milk
From a bottle; bright new sheep for the grasslands
Tumble; Adam and Eve are still at last
(Their breath marks on the glass). This is
The world that they were born for, if not born into.

Here is the woman, here is the man.
Here is the earth in the palm of our hand.

Sciomancy

It is the shape you make, the kind of sun
You don't let fall that tells me what I need.
You see, the ground is scorched with emptiness.

You will be subject to the wind. The earth
Will never have you. You lingered here. Your lover
Will leave once you are nothing but apple core.

It's gotten so no longer do I need
The shadow. I can read its former place,
As if you sat in grass and left just moments

Ago. You want to know the future, tell
The past. It is the trace you left on time,
The way shadows are our temporary stain

On the world. See how even in your sways,
Your slightest twitches, you have heralded
The long road of all your misdecisions, the loss

Of all your better possibilities.
It is a bottomless box. Stare if you like.
But you, who think that God has fled your side,

Bent double as you are, won't find him in
The dirt. This, I know more about than most—
You cannot find the absent in the absence.

We Have Our Inheritance

At Eliot's house in Boston we kissed. I put
My fingers [Power lines crisscrossed the street] —
The tigers, restless for their sides of meat,
Stood on hind legs and peeked through the door shut
To keep them outside. This was Providence,
The Roger Williams Zoo where we first knew
There are no bars. But there are bars: a few
Words on old signs said so, and *after this*

Our exile were we inside then, or both,
Like the folded-in skin of your open mouth?
We watched the tigers ineffectually scratch
The trees, each swipe sounding like a clicking latch.
— [made a net for the sky] on your buttons, but,
Touching the house, you sighed, the way was shut.

Tower of Babel

You're in the country of a thousand tongues.
Landlocked, Landlocked, you say, say, like a bird
Of some other paradise (Langue d'Oïl? Langue d'Oc?).
You are locked in by the locked-in; the word

From here is sealed. The insulated heaven
Won't let itself be sieged so easily.
Forever uncompleted the tower stands,
Its skirts surrounded by phonemic debris.

Amid a crowd of the once unionized,
But now adrift, you stand, where each wind-blown
Sand grain is carving vowels into new shapes.
Searching for ways to speak that won't disown

Your soul from its inheritance, as if
The right or wrong words held the balance scale
Of everything, you open the chrysalid
Of your tongue and hope the butterfly will sail

To the right ear. But you know, after all,
We'll not be listening to one another,
But forging ahead, tongues extended like snakes,
Seeking in the air, not sound, but cover.

Aristaeus

The gods destroyed his hives.

Honey and wax clung to the super's hives,
The bees suppressed with almond scent, and sent
Disoriented down into the colony
So we could harvest what they'd given us.

In Pharaoh's time, the doctors covered cuts
In honey, balm to kill bacteria.
Thousands of years, the honey's still unspoiled.
As are the wounds, and O to lick them clean.

The Snow Globe of Drowning Bears

A shelf of ice breaks off
And summers to the south,
Bread torn from a loaf
And dipped into the mouth.

The children drowned in the kelp
Off the Kentucky coast.
Blesséd are those born
With genes for webbed toes.

At harvest time in Canada
Heft the pomegranates
Into baskets, like the whole
World he's got in his hands.

Shake it, please, and send us scattering.

Letter to the Unconverted

And what would you say if I told you the deer had spoken?
    Two animals, we were face to face in the wood
And stopped each other dead in the last light
    Of day, the cold coming down the hillside,

Descending as ash that would preserve us like this,
    Clay jars that could crumble at the lightest push,
Here in this moment, or the next (that haven
    Of the already dead), crumbling in a flash

Of powder, still too late to catch the spirit
    Escaped, wild and full of unknown sound,
Virgin language to the eager ear,
    Beautiful unearthly distance unwound.

What would you say if I told you this? The light
    Detached like a ghost, expanded before it broke
With bark and dirt, and watched the two of us
    Solidify. What would you say? The deer spoke.

The Queen Died of Grief

What makes a story: *why*.
The queen's pain burst the royal cloak
        And left her to die.

The subtle glancing stroke
Of the pen changes the story's shape:
        From the royal oak

She hanged herself, the rope
Made of hairs from her adorer,
        Who gave her a slip

Of a ring, the queen's before her,
Under the very tree, which went
        From seed to bower

In the family line's descent.
Surely, the queen died. But her grief
        Was a thing spent

On more than death: the sheaf
Of her days loosely held by politics
        And disbelief:

The kingdom rotted, the cliques
Took over, foresting their schemes
        And subtle tricks

Because of all her dreams
Come true there were no children. She sighed
Deeply, whole streams

Of them, until she died.
The queen is dead. Nothing to see
Here. She tried

To hold onto memory
Too long, as we did, who should have known
How the story

Ends.

Polar Bear at the Edge of a Hole in the Ice

What is white in morning, whiter
In the afternoon, and whiter still
When the sun's sway over the world
Seems a thing out of a past life?
Nothing the world will say appalls him,
For he can see for miles across
The wilderness. There he is a sphinx
Of ice awaiting travelers
To ask his solitary question.
A buddha gazing at the ice's navel,
Dispensing flakes of wisdom to melt
Upon your thickening tongue. A sentry
Waiting for what the sea would hiccup
Out of the O of blue before him—
No hibernation until the seal
Breaks the surface of the water.

He stares—the blue stares back.

Atlantis

Remember the way the water slipped over the city's edge.
Rain collected in pools with other water, seeing and
forgetting everything, including you and the crumbling
columns of your bones. Forget your old desire. The city was
obliterated, just as if by rebels who said *me*, and then *me*
once more. There is no distance needed, only recognition.
Remember the way the water slipped over the city's edge
was like a girl's crucifix falling from her neck.

Christmas with Kings

Valley of the Kings, Egypt, December 25, 1999

Here, where kings have come to rest, we are
The day's first tourists, sun just a white glare.
Robed men perch in the rocks above the valley,
Watchdogs or worse, as we enter an open tomb.

Cold walls have lost most of their paint, the flecks
Of sky flaked off now mingling with the sand.
The ceiling's yellow stars in the blue sky
Almost nothing, as if obscured by smoke.

The way to heaven was through the earth, the kings
All knew. Surrounded by gifts, wrapped in cloth,
Wanting safe passage in their human way
From the old dispensation into the new.

Christ knew it too; would wrap himself in skin
And hide himself inside himself. And only
After burial could he be raised.
The sun through the shaft is seen the whole way back.

I'm hoping for others when we reach the top,
Expecting terror from the watchers: thieves,
Shepherds, angels, depending on the story
This turns out to be. They've disappeared.

Which leaves us in doubt and sleeved in dust
From kicked-up wind. More tourists move in and out

Of open tombs. Whatever made these gods
Human is over the peaks and untraceable,

Yet leaves its mark indelibly with us,
Messenger, message, folding into one.
Like the dust we are on a windstorm lifted,
That which is sky is now dirt, and the dirt sky.

Termination Shock

For David Citino

*The Voyager 1 spacecraft has arrived at the boundary of
the solar system and is flying into a region of space that
has never been explored before.*

—Kate Tobin, CNN

The Voyager has reached the end of all
We know. Escaped the grips of Pluto, sailed
On solar wind to termination shock,
The outer door of our nine-room mobile home.
And what beyond? Into the clicking code
Of aliens or swallowed by the mouth
Of God? And will a ring of angels greet
Our proxy, sing hosannas at its coming?
Here is our robot pilgrim sent to do
The hard work of investigating what
Is waiting on the other side of life.
They say that it will reach the nearest star
In forty thousand years. Inside its belly,
It carries comfort: *once I had a mom
And dad who smiled—they send their greetings.* Will
It see the light as its aging circuits fail?
Even in deep space there is nothing but questions.
All this comes to we *will go on* in some
Way or other, leaving one sun for
Another, shocked to have to end, and shocked
Further by the what that's coming next.

And yet we have not reached the great below.
Two miles underneath the ice are buried

The lakes and islands of Antarctica.
Out of reach by any human drill,
What beings might play there? A kingdom preserved
Like a room in some museum of our end.
Boats wait at the dock. One day this will all
Unfreeze and we can sail ourselves
Into the last interior, a shock
Of spray from that icy water way down deep
Where the soul is, borne on a breeze that pulls us
Inward until there is no place but the next.

Crossing the Border

In a vineyard after snowfall I'm convinced it's an army of skeletons marching across Denmark. The one leaf still clinging is the General's feather, or the single hair you left in my brush.

We managed to get you in the ground before it froze. In the spring, you'll be the melting snow. All I have now is the typewriter. I tore its keys off and bloodied my hands on its bones, my play stuck in intermission.

//

And sometimes, in a shop, the mirrors
Were still dizzy with your presence and, startled, gave back
My too-sudden image.

—Rainer Maria Rilke

The Old Balladeer Retires after Too Many Years of Hoping the Woman at Table 12 Would Understand He Was Singing to Her All That Time

If asked, I will refuse to sing.
    No dram or draught will draw
The lyric out of me. I'll keep it
    Like gravel in my craw.

Consider this tongue silent, lost
    To beat and to vibration,
A dead hand useless to your suit
    As clubs to procreation.

Although it seems like we're still young,
    You've come in here for years,
Your blonde gone gray, your gin gone dry.
    The smoke between us clears.

Once, you looked, those wet eyes raised,
    I was certain that you heard
My veiled confession, but then up flew
    The glimmer like a bird.

My voice will slip as if full of sleep
    Down to the back of my heart.
Asylum there will seem a safe
    Untippable apple cart.

No requests tonight, no rings
    Thrown at my feet for more.

There is no kingdom left to me
    In the word-hoard of before.

Why should I begrudge you this?
    You've made your choice, and leaning
That way, I knew you only came
    For melody, not meaning.

The song that paved the *via dulce*
    Is the one you want to hear.
You think I make it with a voice,
    I made it with a spear.

The Little Sphinx

Luxor Temple

With his semi-automatic machine gun
He waves me over. He's a Tourist Policeman,
But it's still a gun. He leads me through an arch,
Around a corner to some antechamber
Guidebooks don't remember. Arabic
To me is a lizard that darts behind the rocks—
I'll never catch it—and his English is
A mix of McDonald's and *Miami Vice*.
He points to a statue of a sphinx the size
Of a German shepherd, though it's possible
I'm being told to get down on my knees.
But really he is playing the tour guide
And wants me to shoot it with my camera,
And so I do. He smiles. I hand him five
Egyptian pounds *baksheesh*. He hands me back
My life.
      How American to be afraid.
To make him someone who would kill. Or maybe
It's only human to think we are our own
Most impending danger. We who know
The desert mirage and still walk toward it.
I wonder if the sphinx will bark its question
And make me answer for myself. What are
Two legs at noon good for if not to go
Somewhere else and know that somewhere else?
Though this keeper of an alleyway was tossed
In a corner of a ruined temple, it's still
A kind of crossroads here, two languages

Looking for a way to pass each other
Without first reaching for a sword.
We have done little to quell the sphinx's anger.
He must still want to crack his stone encasement,
Stretch his jaw and tear us savagely.
See the punctures of his canines, how
Like bullet holes, both empty and intrusive.

My Daughter as the Angel Gabriel in the Tableau Vivant of Van Grap's Annunciation

I gave birth to an angel, which is wrong
Twice over, though it's hard to resist the thought.
I neither gave birth to her (just ask my wife)
Nor is she an angel (just ask her rattled teacher).
And yet there she is, in white and wings,
Long lily in one hand, the other held
To Mary as God's proxy. Scrap semantics,
Embrace your sentimentality, I say,
Despite the better angels of my nature.
She is still as she never is at home.
Still enough to be one of the host.
I do not want responsibility
For words, so let my daughter be an angel,
Let the painting live as if a stone were rolled.
It is the ultimate *trompe l'oeil* on stage,
They are there, and they are not, the way
I could pull back the curtain on this sight
To show you all the brushstrokes, that the child
On stage is not my daughter, but may be
An angel yet, one of those who is there
And not there in the corners of our eyes,
Which this little play has meant to fool,
Not out of any malice for the viewer
But to make a world in which I have a daughter,
Because I wish I did, and never will.

Paradis

After a photograph by Charles Marville

The street is empty, paving stones
Crowd the vein that runs through the photograph.
The lamp is unlit that leads the way (too narrow
For echo) between the street's silent houses.
The scene has a swept look, as if the light
Had pasteurized the place, so now it is
Beautiful only, the way a painted scene
Of fruit in landscape is, beautiful
And charmed, as if all that were left behind
Was sleep and standing water for reflection.

Whitewater Rafting

We like to toy with death. On a pleasure cruise
(Wet bar, a show at ten, a purser *plus*
Named Fanny), life was nothing but good news,
But good news is hardly ever worth the fuss.

So then came boredom, and we jumped off-board
In a life raft, headed downstream, drifting
Along the soda bubble current toward
An unknown destiny. A boatman's grifting

Some virgin rafters—*a penny for a ride,*
He says as we wave freely past the dock.
How he scowls from beneath his hood. *Who died?*
We joke—he cracks, laughs like an alarm clock.

Ripples erupt and suddenly the spray
Hits our faces like a buckshot round.
We paddle hard and bail, but cannot stay
The river's thirst to swallow us whole—downed

Like a colored pill. Through rapids, a rock juts—
We wedge against it like a camel caught
In the needle's noose. We hang a moment (our guts
Tell us it's a chance to flee) before the knot

Unbinds and we're shoved through by force of pent-
Up water, a mad dash across the waves
Ready to go under as a rent
Opens in the craft, but a sandbar saves

Us and we wade to shore. It's bleached to bone.
The crowds emerge from the dark island's wood.
Will they jeer us for coming on our own?
Their news: by our own hands, we're here for good.

Meditations of the Tomb Painters

1.

The pyramid has fallen in my nightmare,
And I am trapped inside of Pharaoh's tomb.
The yellow ceiling stars crashed down to earth
To the cenotaphs below. The beer jars cracked
Around his sarcophagus, ushabtis dashed
To the dust, canopic organs under stone.
The words of Osiris broken, the sun-boat scuttled,
Split entrails of Hathor are anyone's to read.
In some hard sentence on our labor, here
Are all the years of work collapsed around
The skin of god inside a scroll of linen,
Sealed from the silent, desiccated air.
A thousand nights gone by I've never had
This dream before: The king and I are dead,
With sand and rock and empire on our head.

2.

No king will cross without my services.
A recitation of the words I write
Calls the afterlife to open. My touch
Is feather-light on the glyphs whose pattern will
Be as the stones across a stream. No drop
Of water will undo his drying skin.

For practice, I paint them on my walls at home.
It is not sacred, but it hides the question
What golden boat will come for me?
The words are fog below the cliffs and I
Am quarried stone. When I die, plaster me
With papyrus reeds and leave me for the bees.

3.

We salted oil to keep down the smoke
And so there was no border between the flame
And the black air. An oval on the wall
Was all we had—a small sun where we fixed
The images for Pharaoh's passing through.
The gauze was being twisted as we worked.

And where was he now, having died and not
Yet risen, incubating, pigment mixing
With water? It is known where he will be;
I have foretold his story on the wall.
What middle country holds his soul these days,
The seventy I have to paint his world:

Here is Osiris touching Pharaoh's head;
Here is the boat across the lonely river;
Here is my heart in paint, a stowaway
Inside the art that only God would see.

Adam Gifts Eve with a Session of Boudoir Photography

The spark is gone. She said this, this cliché—
Its innocuousness struck him all the harder.
He needed innovation. He would portray
Himself as in a secluded bower—boudoir
Photography sessions bought one for the pair.
He might have pierced a body part to make
Her belly ring a partner, or carved her fair
Impression on his skin (he loved that snake
Tattoo around her ankle), but he chose
This method to renew their love. He felt
Like Adam rising into grace—and rose
To the occasion, fumbled with his belt,
Recalled that first picture in the rented tux.
The flashbulb popped. He thought, *fiat lux.*

Hey, You've Got to Hide Your Love Away

Hartsville, TN. (AP) G & L Garden Center responded to
complaints by covering up the classical-style statues with
stylish, two-piece crimson velvet sarongs.

They've been converted from a group
    Of blushing goddesses
To Victoria's Secret models — made
    The more alluring by
A pair of velvet wraps — here
    And here.
What I once passed as garden junk
    I jam my brakes for now,
Heeding at last my wife's requests
    To decorate the house.
Some kids are peeking — lifting up
    To spy what's underneath.
The bravest raise the bottoms. The hidden
    Is sexier, and it
Is scarier, as Hitchcock shuts
    The door in *Frenzy*, leaves
Behind the killer with Miss Victim,
    And pulls the camera down
The stairs and out of the house. What we
    Imagine is always worse,
Or better, perfect curve of a breast
    Made from good chiseling —
How easy for that knife to sink
    Too deeply. The curtain rises
To reveal Pygmalion's masterpiece
    Is real, raw skin unmarbled
And marvelous.

Somewhere in the Mediterranean

At the bottom lies the statue of a boy
That never made its way from Greece to Rome,
Losing itself to salt, which might drift home
Or flow down to Hades like blood at Troy
Passed into the sea. The water's wake
Was a mouth always opening to tell
Its secrets, but now, the engine still,
It snapped shut before what's below could speak.

How sure are you it isn't your reflection?
The deckhands' shouts in Arabic are charms,
Perhaps, to stay afloat, when a course correction
Won't do. If you dove in, you might not drown,
And find out what he has to say, his arms
Spread out and waiting for you to swim down.

A Generic Pietà

I'm sure it was in Florence, but which church
I can't remember now; each held their light
So much the same, in flat disks you could stand in,
And every sound was paper thin. In the air,
The dust motes carried few if any stories
And kept the holy hall blank with mystery.

And there, past the confused light of stained glass,
Fracturing someone's martyrdom to pieces,
Crouched Mary, her boy heaped in her lap.
I had seen this before and known the look
Of difficult pity on the mother, strained
By loss and gain, and the slackened face of Christ.

The artist must have seen what life was drawn
Out of the stone by Masters with the power
Of Moses and his dowsing rod, that he
Could not exhume this same ferocity.
Could he feel the anonymity
Creeping over his flesh like a wasting disease?

And yet, in service to his patron, his Lord,
His soul, he sweated out the days and the light's
Unmysterious cast on his thinning stone;
Because this was all he knew, for months he hacked
Away at marble with all his might and stood
There weeping at its all too common beauty.

Chagall in Heaven

Chagall went up but never came down,
The story goes, rising out
Of his body as his body rose.
The gates that parted for Chagall
Were not the same as for the nurse,
Who must have inhaled his last breath.
Poetic, one might say, that since
He painted rising as if it
Were natural as gravity,
He should die this ordered way.
A justice that defies the way
Of things on Earth, as if we said
The nurse never had to exhale,
And a body could keep going up.

The Enemies of Poise

Are legion. Lack of Confidence will cloud
The air around you for certain, if allowed,
Like a bad batch of petaled potpourri.
Look at your hand. You're shaking as before, see?
Back then you weren't convicted, so justice weighed
Against you, tipped the scales and then waylaid
Any plans you might have had, had you
Any strength to run the tables through,
But your extended sword is held by Weakness
(The limp-wristed shake his favorite sign of meekness . . .).
Your nervous tongue's a dolphin that breaks the water
Too fast, then dives before you can recover.
She gazes blankly like a coral reef
And there you sit on edge and deep in grief.
Your hands flit like a hyperactive kid,
Puppeteered by Fidget from your Id.
Sloth and Want are a pair of foes, fraternal
Twins who bend and slacken posture, your lines all
Deparalleled into an engineer's
Worst nightmare. Who would trust your tracks? She steers
Toward the bullish fellow, and, although
His nose is red, at least this charming beau
Has color. You've gone so ghostly pale that she
You're looking over, overlooks your plea,
And leaves you chewing, like bad paté, your past.
Overanxious then underwhelming, at last
The heart slumps to the liver, couches there
Until it's half its size, a small repair

Or two you think, then head for a drink, descend
Until the worst of demons, the Arch-Fiend,
The great reductionist, Depression, lies
And sinks his weight into your weakening thighs
Shrinking your size before you know deception
Has inked into your veins, a soft injection,
A spinal tap that curves your spine into
A question mark, the *trompe l'oeil* that new
Ideas you have are graced with. Though you tell
Yourself, the world, that everything is well
(And yes, from dark below the sky is bright),
How fast the friends, the jobs, the loves take flight
Because your shaking hand, your shaking fist
Hits only air and all you've missed.

You Put Your Right Hand In, You Take Your Left Hand Out

Remember when we found
Our right our left? Looking in our mirrors,
Kids with elephant-big surprise, traders in a new world,
Its natural laws yet undefined, we fiddled dextrously
With air to see our moves reversed,
        Then touched the glass
Because we thought we could be immersed
In our own image, but something sinister beckoned restlessly:
We'd been embarrassed by that reflexive huckster. Our minds whirled
At buying left for right, and became wayfarers
Lost to a common ground.

And so we're left with our
Two hands, and their palms staring back at us,
Say, like the *Schatzbehalter* hands, the fingers covered with Christ
And saints like tattoos to mark your loyalties. If you would stow
Them, you'd have to make a fist. So then,
        Dressed like stained glass
We carry a cathedral in
Our hands, and in the mirror now, our left hand seems to know
Exactly what the right is doing, and what is sacrificed
Is tallied on the eternal abacus,
Our book of one right hour.

Merry Christmas, Titan

The Cassini spacecraft will release the piggybacked Huygens probe towards Titan's atmosphere on Christmas Day.

—BBC

To you we bring our knowledge, our invention,
Our metal. May it have safe harbor in
Your liquid hydrocarbon sea or warmth
In the fissures of your ice. Beneath the methane
May it find new measure for an old
Sense of weight. Our humble messenger,
Which might have seemed a star at first, and then
A wave of light, is made of stuff you're not
Familiar with, but someday soon won't it come
To seem so? That's the wish we pack onboard.
We're planning ahead, you see, in case we need
To darken your door, our words and our few things,
With news of some other place we once called home.

Memento Amori

Burkittsville, Maryland

I'm obsessed with a little angel,
Contorting myself to get the angle,
While Cindy wanders through the stone,
Snapping away in the good sun
The day ends with, rays like a lid
Almost shut. What are the dead
That we cross their graves for art?
Leaves drift at the base, the flowers rot,
Spiders cast. Photos are a skull.
I take the angel. Behind the hill,
Cindy's disappeared. What light
Remains I leave to find her out.

Bear

Along the trail, I drag my shadow behind me
As the sun burns into my forehead. The woods
Of Virginia do not move, except everywhere,
Slowly. Ahead, the stillness is the same.
Even the trees are bending with the weight
Of air. I've walked for miles and yet seen nothing.
No scurryings, only wind-howls at cliff-edges,
Where stunted pines like suicides look down.

Down into the valley, the light dulls.
What's left luminous is the moss in shadow.
And in the river basin, among the deadfall,
Scruff sparks in the brush and out comes a bear,
Running into the woods. I stand amazed.
Like darkness exposed to sunlight. An empty bowl
To water. The footbeats leave their echoes.

Adam's Tongue

And here, at last, is what you've all been waiting for,
The tongue of Adam, pink and fleshy, sweet as attar,

Kept behind glass for centuries. And while the world
Raged on it has kept its silent vigil, here chapeled

For all to come and see the first communicant
With God, the Holy Name's first instrument.

What treasure compares to this? Teresa in Avila?
St. Martin's cloak? Or Peter's tongue, with its denials?

And so we have come to keep it here, past the altar
For sacrifice, the stone confessional, the censer-

Smoke rising, here ensconced with the bottles of nard
And the monks' hairshirts, and the funeral cards.

Just how it came to be here is not known, but legend
Has it that Cain returned to see his father's end,

Crept in the night to cut out Adam's tongue and carry
It as a token of his fall; perhaps mere story,

But was Cain surprised by the incorruptibility
Of the tongue, its failure to shrivel, blacken to a tiny

Coal-dark flake of soul? This was still body, *father's*,
Live with every spark of care. Holding it, it dithers.

Here it is, the first of blessers, the first of kissers,
The first of namers, the first of acquiescers.

The cost to look is free, but there is a box to donate,
For those of you whose hands, unlike this tongue, aren't
      mute.

Stone Goddess

Her statue. In the broken garden. Leaves
Obliterated. Fingers missing, chip
Out of her stomach. In the folded eaves

Of her hair, silence sluices through. A drip
Suffers down the arc of her downcast stare.
Trees bowering, folding in. Rotting tulip

Laid at the placard. What it says. Stained altar.
To think of those who come to worship her.

The Nature Trail

The Eden Historic Park welcomes all visitors between the hours of seven a.m. and dusk. There is convenient parking located next to the Park Headquarters and Gift Shop. Our Ranger Angel is always on duty at the gate to answer any questions you might have, and to point out a few sights to see along the way. Catch him on the right day, and he might show you his antique sword.

Starting from the gate, there's a slight upgrade
Where you'll encounter (1) a dead fig tree,
    The branches splayed
In a gesture of combustion. Further on,
    The path winds past a field of scree

And down to the spring (2) from which are drawn
Four rivers: Gihon, Tigris, and Euphrates,
    And dry Pishon
(Too much was taken quenching oil fires —
    Too late our minds divine what Fate sees

In its telescopic view). The waiting choirs
Of trees project to (3) the Naming Stone,
    Where Adam's quires
Were filled with every appellation he
    Fired in the kiln of his brain,

The animals lined and blessed with his decree.
The trail leads upwards to the highest rise
    In the park. See
How the path opens to a circular grove
    (4) where the sunlight falls slantwise

On two trees, (5) The Tree of Life, which wove
Its roots with (6) The Tree of Knowledge of Good

And Evil, but strove
Somehow to separate, and so it grew
    At an angle, and for years the wood

Has leaned away as if its sister's taboo
Were a lit match. As you pass by the pair,
    Notice the two
Burns (7) on the trunk: cuneiform
    Inscriptions, older than the Sumer

Dialect. Deciphering this swarm
Of wedge-shaped letters has been difficult;
    We think the triform
Marks are those for A + E; however,
    In academic circles, the tumult

That romantic notion sparked began to sever
Several ties between the Park and the field
    Of linguists, clever
Though it may be. The trail continues down;
    Through here the fallen leaves will yield

To solid ground as you, lost in the gown
Of light that shifts through the clerestory,
    A new meltdown
Of body into fire, descend and keep
    Descending, for this trail, like the story,

Does not loop back, but reaches to a deep
Where light is sweeter for reaching further in
    Where you will steep
Until your body has blended into light,
    Burns forever and is not burned.

Your Art History

1. First Lesson

The first thing I ever heard from you
Was how to paint the Savior dead.

I felt unseated, struck like Mary
At the angel's visitation,

And fell in love with your voice. Here
Was prophecy: I sensed the words

Shook you as much as they shook me.
But the foretold means nothing if none

Can read what's on the summer air
And what is not: against the dark

A flash of fireflies, a speck
Of water on the brightest day.

2. Interpretation

Here you are the Corinthian Maid,
Trying to get your lover into the sun
To trace his shadow. Always he must go,
Always you stay. How you will learn to love
The rock you drew on when he's gone.
Born out of need to keep at least a ghost
Of our loves, the history of art is this:
The bitter kiss of chalk left on your lips
When stone is film plate and adored.
Forget the process, love the aftertaste.

When Adam left to tend his olives,
You were left to bear his image.
His knee-high boys with jelly-covered fingers
Grasped your skirt and marked their territory.
The jelly stains were little hearts all over you.
No woman had ever been so loved, you told yourself,
And scratched a stick into the ground.

3. *Case Study* (The Annunciation *by Jan van Eyck*)

Here she stands stained blue
And ready to divide
Into a copy of God,

Who focuses His light
Through the window-lens — her name
Projected upside-down

As if the painter knew
Years hence all newlyweds
Would be thus joined and sainted.

4. Inspiration

Right now you are afield
Taking impossible photographs
    Of a wedding—someone you
Once loved, and someone else in white.
    The invitation plain
And on the level; still, you wonder
If this is a fiction you're creating.

Look at the image reborn
In the chemical bath, the darkness drawn
    Out of the white, and fixed
Forever. Though maybe some time later
    You'll find a small square emptied
Of its memories, the way her dark
    Hair loosened from the veil
And spilled over the dress, his tie
    Undone and hanging down
His wine-stained shirt-front as they fall
Into the car and disappear.

Go. The world is nothing
But waiting for the light to burn
    All the images
Of what it will be like henceforth,
    And what it used to be.
Like a ring, glinting inside the paper,
The twist of silver tells us so.

The End

Mizen Head, Co. Cork

Where Ireland loses to Atlantic waves.
A finger in the water. Past each sheep-
Infested curve we've come to see the end.
Far enough the Romans never made
This coast. Past Crookhaven, Cork, the port of Cobh.
I feel the flag pin push into the map.
My father's camera rings his neck. Gray hair
Like seafoam on his head, yellow and brown
In mine like seaweed. No one else is there
When we arrive, not even lighthouse keepers.
Late winter clouds are nestling in the mud.
After a gate we need to hurdle—rust
Crumbles off in our hands and turns to powder—
There is one bridge out to the lighthouse rock.
I follow my father in, until the fog
Makes of distinction absolutely nothing.

Notes

Epigraph to Part I

Ben Howard, *Father of Waters* (Omaha, NE: Abattoir Editions, 1979).

Chiaroscuro

Caravaggio's *The Taking of Christ* (1602) was thought lost by the eighteenth century. The painting hanging in the dining room of the Society of Jesus in Dublin, Ireland, since the early 1930s had long been considered a copy by Gerard van Honthorst, also known as Gerard of the Nights, one of Caravaggio's Dutch followers. A cleaning in 1990 revealed that the supposed copy was actually the original. (National Gallery of Art, Washington, D.C.; http://www.nga.gov/caravbr-1.shtm)

Aristaeus

For the story, please see Virgil's fourth *Georgic*.

Termination Shock

Though the poem was written before David Citino's death, and not meant *in memoriam*, I include it here now in his memory.

Epigraph to Part II

Rainer Maria Rilke, *The Selected Poetry of Rainer Maria Rilke*, trans. Stephen Mitchell (New York: Vintage, 1989).

You Put Your Right Hand In, You Take Your Left Hand Out

Schatzbehalter hands — The image is from a religious treatise by Stefan Fridolin (published by Anton Koberger in 1491), which contained ninety-six full-page woodcuts of biblical subjects by Michael Wolgemut and his school (which included Albrecht Dürer). The book's original full title is *Schatzbehalter der wahren Reichtümer des Heils (Treasury of the True Riches of Salvation)*.

Chagall in Heaven

I am indebted to Jessica Hamilton for this story.

Your Art History

Owes very much to Cynthia Hoffman.

/